Eva Maria Leszner

KNITTED LACE DESIGNS OF
HERBERT NIEBLING

TRANSLATION OF GESTRICKTE SPITZENDECKEN

SECOND PRINTING

CHARTS EDITED AND REVISED BY MARY FRANCES WOGEC

LACIS
PUBLICATIONS

This book is a translation of the original German language work titled

GESTRICKTE SPITZENDECKEN by Eva Maria Leszner
first published by Rosenheimer Verlagshaus in 1986 with ISBN 3-475-52497-X.
© 1986 Rosenheimer Verlagshaus GmbH & Co. KG, Rosenheim, Germany

Photo on page 8 is credited to S.B. Muller-Schilling, Freiburg
All other photos included in this book have been taken by E.M. and D. Leszner

Chart editing and revisions for this edition: Mary Frances Wogec
Assisted by: Eve-Isabelle Charbonneau, Yenju Chen, Maia Discoe, Wendy Gilmore, Wes Thyberg and
the members of the *Yahoo Niebling Lace Knitters Group*
English translation: Yasmin Syed and Mary Frances Wogec

This Second Printing incorporates the errata for the initial printing,
correcting errors that were, identified on pages 28, 29, 52 and 91.

THIS EDITION PUBLISHED BY

LACIS
PUBLICATIONS
3163 ADELINE STREET
BERKELEY, CA 94703

© 2009 English text and chart revisions,
Lacis Publications, Lacis.com

ISBN 978-1-891656-87-3

Baby bonnet, Hessen, late 19th c., knitted lace with white cotton thread.
From the Collection of Folk art in Hessen, Museum Veste Otzberg

Introduction

Knitting - everyone thinks first of warm, fashionable winter sweaters, of hats, scarves, and socks, secondly, of attractive vests and tops in the latest colors and designs. Whether fashionable or classical, whether in wool, cotton, or other fibers, we always think first of garments when we hear the word "knitting".

There seem to be worlds separating these utilitarian textiles and paper-thin starched lace creations. Lace – many people will first think of crocheting, then some will remember that particularly fine lace can also be created with bobbins or needles. The laces presented in this book, however, are ordinary works of knitting, which are worked with a set of double point needles or a circular needle. These knitted tablecloths are commonly referred to as "art knitting" (Kunststricken), a term which became prevalent in the nineteen twenties. It is an appropriate term when you consider the completed tablecloths: exquisitely fine filigree patterns which seem all the more artful the finer the thread from which they were magically created. Nevertheless, I find the term misleading, because the technique is simple, not at all the high art of knitting that the name and the beautiful result would lead you to believe. Socks and gloves are, I think, far more difficult to knit. With knitted tablecloths, there are only knits and very rarely purl stitches, yarn overs, and increasing and decreasing. They are always knitted in the round. Knitted lace tablecloths are therefore a simple piece of needlecraft that should be easy for anyone who has ever knitted a sweater with a lace pattern. The techniques are presented in small steps on pages 9-16. All you need in order to knit these beautiful tablecloths yourself is crochet thread instead of wool or cotton yarn, and the courage to try something new and to put beauty before practicality in knitting.

Knitting is perhaps the most popular of the needle crafts in which thread is looped with the aid of one or more needles in such a way that fabric is created. Related to knitting are crochet and filet crochet, tatting, macrame, bobbin lace, and needle lace. As far back as antiquity, needlecrafts of this sort were produced. Ancient Egyptians, Coptic Christians, and Greeks used all kinds of techniques of this sort. When interpreting funerary finds, often tiny pieces of felted materials, and images from ancient vases and reliefs, scholars seldom agree on what technique is represented in each individual case.

Depending on whether the author writes about knitting, crocheting, or knotting, the earliest archaeological finds are always claimed for the technique that the author is writing about. Be that as it may, techniques similar to knitting have been around for more then three thousand years. Knitting needles of bone were found in the grave of a Thuringian duchess around 300 A.D., and iron knitting needles in a Merovingian grave around 500 A.D. Beginning in the 13th century, evidence of knitting accumulates, especially in Spain and Italy. By the 16th century at the latest, knitting as a craft had spread all across Europe. At first, only men exercised this craft, and they set themselves laws and regulations like any other guild. For example, in 1529, the guild of sock knitters was founded in Paris, and in 1590, the first guild of knitters of hosiery in Berlin. Knitters, who belonged to the trade of weavers, produced socks, hosiery, gloves and caps. In Italy in the 17th century, particularly ornate patterned knit wares were produced by the yard, from which jackets and vests were tailored. Germany and Austria were famous for their knitted wool carpets.

There were silk knitters and wool knitters; the material determined the fineness of the end product: on the one hand there were fine silk stockings and gloves, knitted with pearls and gold and silver threads for the aristocracy and ecclesiastical hierarchy. On the other hand, garments from coarser material were produced for ordinary people.

But the craftsmen of the guilds were not the only knitters. In areas where sheep raising was important, for example in Scotland and Ireland, a thriving cottage industry developed. Men, women and children knitted for their own needs but primarily to generate urgently needed additional income.

While crochet, which developed at the same time as knitting, always remained a handcraft, the first knitting machine was invented in 1589 by the Englishman William Lee. Queen Elizabeth, who prohibited the use of machines in order not to endanger the livelihood of handknitters, could delay progress but not stop it. It took only a hundred years until knitting machines replaced handknitters. Only in a few remote areas where traditional patterns were cultivated did the handknitting industry remain alive and productive into the 19th century.

The more commercial knitting was taken over by machines, the more hand knitting became a female craft for the household's own consumption—as a pastime for the wives of the wealthy, and for the production of inexpensive warm clothing for the less wealthy. In principle this has remained so to this day, except that the number of those who have time and leisure for knitting has multiplied exponentially.

Since the 17th century, lace and its manifold techniques have been known in Europe as a fashion accessory for the decoration of clothing and other textiles. Lace is primarily a border and a decorative embellishment. Laces became broader and more ornate as techniques of lacemaking were refined. Soon large collars, cuffs, tablecloths, and fabric for clothing were produced with lace techniques.

While centers for bobbin lace and needle lace developed in Italy, France, and Belgium, the techniques for producing lace knitting and lace crochet were refined in Germany, England, and the Netherlands. This development was furthered by the import of cotton from the colonies, which could be spun into very fine threads. Wool is only suited for lace knitting when spun very fine and double plied, a time consuming technique which was almost exclusively practiced in the Shetland Islands. The fine knitted lace shawls of these islands were a highly sought item of trade because of their fineness and the wide range of patterns.

Knitted lace always seems lighter and airier than crocheted lace. Due to the difference in technique, knitting requires only a third of the yarn needed for crochet. Knitted lace is therefore more similar in effect to the more expensive bobbin lace than crocheted lace. Outside the Shetland Islands, however, lace knitting was never commercially viable, but from the beginning was practiced primarily in the home.

In the 18th and early 19th centuries, at the high point of female handcrafts, tablecloths and doilies, collars, cuffs and jabots, but above all children's bonnets (see pl. on p. 4) and christening gowns were knitted in beautiful lace patterns. These were knitted on very thin wire needles and often worked with sewing thread, resulting in a very fine pattern while still producing a sturdy fabric.

Knitted lace tablecloths--such as those presented in this book--found new popularity in the nineteen twenties. There were no circular needles at that time (these were introduced only in the thirties), but knitting needles became stronger and made it possible to work more quickly and to effect an especially light, gossamer look. Above all, however, it was only in the 20th century that charts were introduced for lace patterns. These make lace knitting much easier, and it is a pity that even today there are no standardized

Hebert Niebling (1905-1966)
A career artist, devoting his life to the development and production of artistic lace knitting designs.

symbols, and that they are not used for all knitting patterns.

The first patterns for lace tablecloths were simple and plain, not at all comparable to the airy and delicate flower patterns presented in this book. Except for the examples on pages 27 and 35, the designs come from the hand of an artist who said about himself, "As the composer writes down the notes that he hears, in the same way I write down the stitches that I see." Herbert Niebling was born in 1905 in Holstein and was already knitting his own socks as a six year old. Knitting and knitting patterns cast their spell over his entire life. When he died in 1966 in Freiburg, he had created thousands of designs for knitted lace over the course of his forty year career and had knitted many tablecloths himself. His most beautiful work was a tablecloth measuring 1 m. by 1 m. Worked in size 200 yarn, it weighs only 30 grams, and is so fine that it can be pulled through a wedding ring, just like the fine shawls from the Shetland Islands.

Herbert Niebling originally wanted to become a businessman, but instead he attended art school in Hamburg. He had an unusual talent: he was able to transfer an image, for example a pot of Alpine violets, directly (that is, without using a drawing or sketch) into a knitting chart for a tablecloth.

While it is already difficult to design a round tablecloth composed of equal wedge-shaped segments freehand, it borders on magic to be able to transpose this pattern into a knitting chart at the same time, keeping in mind both the beautiful design and the mathematics of increases and decreases.

In almost all countries of Europe and also the US, even today the patterns of Herbert Niebling are used. The patterns are timeless and beautiful. For this reason I am happy to be able to introduce to you here patterns that have not yet been published. Without the use of a computer it would be difficult to design new patterns as good as the ones created by this artist in his long career.

Techniques

Knitted tablecloths are worked from the center to the edge in spiral form, in rounds. Depending on the pattern, the first round has 6, 8, or 12 stitches. The number of stitches increases with every round until the knitting reaches approximately 350 stitches for a doily 20 cm. in diameter, and 850 stitches for a large tablecloth 120 cm. in diameter.

The saying "All beginnings are difficult" has a double meaning when it comes to doilies. For one thing, just as with everything else that is new, you have to "get the knack," you have to get used to the technique. But in addition, lace tablecloths are worked from the center. In the center, that is, right at the beginning, it is a bit more difficult because there is so little space for the needles. The larger the rounds become, the easier, faster and simpler the knitting becomes. This is of course a problem, especially for beginners. Do not lose heart right away if it seems difficult at the beginning. After 5 or 6 rounds, it will already be easier, and as soon as you have changed to circular needles, you'll no longer have a problem.

Materials and Equipment

The examples published in this book are all knitted with fine crochet thread, but the tablecloths can just as well be knitted with silk, linen, or cotton thread, or even with sewing thread. Only wool, which is otherwise the usual yarn for knitting, is not suitable. The finer the yarn you choose, the more delicate and more beautiful will be the tablecloth, but unfortunately also the smaller.

Apart from the yarn, you will need a set (= 5) of double point knitting needles and a circular needle in the same size, and in addition, because all knitted doilies are started and finished with a crochet hook, a crochet hook in a size as close as possible to that of the needles.

9

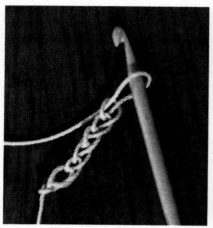  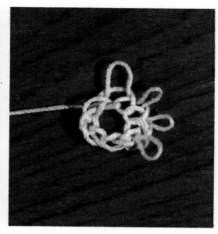

Fig. 1 *Fig. 2* *Fig. 3*

Below the illustrations you will find the diameter of the completed tablecloth, the needle size, the yarn size, and the yarn quantity. If you change the yarn size, you will have to use different size needles accordingly.

The small yarn quantities are not a typo – knitted tablecloths require only a third of the yarn that you would need for a similar crocheted tablecloth. That's why knitted tablecloths have such a delicate appearance.

Casting on the Stitches

The number of cast-on stitches depends on the pattern and is given in each chart. Casting on consists of 5 steps. First, you crochet a chain (*Fig. 1*). Join these into a ring and crochet 3 or 4 slip stitches into the ring, but leave the stitches on the crochet hook *Fig. 2*). Pull out the crochet hook (*Fig. 3*), then put the stitches on a knitting needle, and then crochet the next 3 or 4 slip stitches (*Fig. 4*) until the circle is completed (*Fig. 5*). (I crochet one stitch more than I want to cast on onto the knitting needle [and on the next row, knit the last stitch together with the first stitch to make a smooth join].) Then you continue according to the chart.

In some instructions you cast on a 5- or 6-point star pattern onto 5 or 6 needles in order to have each pattern segment [repeat] on a single needle. I personally find that this is too many needles in too confined a space, and therefore I always distribute the stitches over 3 or 4 needles, even if the number of stitches to be cast on is not divisible by 3 or 4.

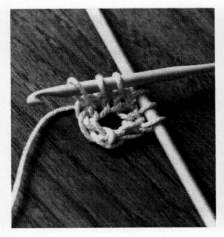

Fig. 4   Fig. 5   Fig. 6

Marking the Beginning of a Row and Changing Needles

The beginning of a row is marked right away in the first round with a clearly visible thread of a different color, which is woven in from round to round. (On one row, you let the thread hang in front of the work, and on the next row, behind it *Fig. 6*.) This way you need not count the stitches in intermediate rounds and you cannot accidentally knit one repeat too few or too many.

As soon as the size of the doily allows, you will change to circular needles. For one thing, they are easier to work with, and for another, they avoid the danger of dropping a stitch from the end of a needle. Circular needles are available in very short lengths.

The Knitting Chart

The knitting charts are easy and use only commonly used symbols which are explained on page 13. As is usual, the knitting charts are read from bottom to top and from right to left. Numbers on the right give the row number.

With the exception of a few cases in which every row is a pattern row, a pattern row is usually followed by an intermediate row which is not given in the chart and is worked only with knit stitches. The only exceptions are in cases when the previous round contains double or triple yarn overs. In the case of 2 yarn overs together in the previous round, in the intermediate row the first yarn over stitch is knitted, the next purled. In the case of 3 yarn overs on the previous round, you alternate knit and purl stitches, but in this case additional stitches often have to be knitted into the 3 yarn overs. These rows

11

are marked with an exclamation point (!), and the number of stitches to be knitted is given in each case.

In order to make counting easier, and to abbreviate the individual rows of the chart as far as possible, several knit stitches one after the other are not given with the symbol [●] but with a numeral (the numeral represents the number of stitches to be knitted).

If a number is underlined, additional stitches have to be knitted at this point (the under-lined numeral represents the number of stitches to be knitted from this one stitch). If a number has a line above it, then stitches are decreased at this point (the numeral with a line over it represents the number of stitches that have to be knitted together as one stitch.)

I find this is easy to remember: if there is only a number, you continue knitting normally; if there is a line above the number – stitches are bundled together here, and above the knitting becomes narrower; if there is a line below the number – the bundle is made from the stitch below, and above the knitting becomes wider.

The larger the tablecloth, the larger the number of stitches in each round, and also the number of signs in the row of the pattern chart. At first glance, the pattern charts with so many signs appear confusing, but when you look at the chart while knitting row by row--as with reading--it becomes clear and is easy to work. Therefore, you should always place an opaque ruler above the row you are currently knitting. Since the chart

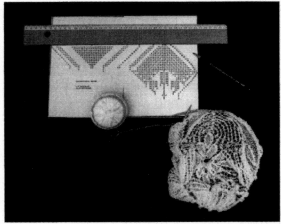

Fig. 7   *Fig. 8*

12

is worked from bottom to top, you will see the previous row but not the following row. In order to find your row when resuming work, or when the ruler has been moved, you should check those rounds which are already knitted with a pencil (*Fig. 7*).

Symbols

A   cast on

●   knit

⑤   several knit stitches in a row: knit as many stitches as the number indicates

⊖   purl

∨   knit through the back loop (twisted stitch)

✕   knit 2 stitches crosswise (Knit into second stitch on left needle but do not slip off, then knit into first stitch and slip off both stitches together.)

○   yarn over

‿   lift the bar between stitches and knit 1 stitch through the back loop (lifted bar increase)

⑤   Knit into this single stitch as many stitches as the number indicates (alternating knit and purl stitches).

◢   knit 2 tog

◣   slip 1 , knit 1, pass the slipped stitch over the knitted stitch, or ssk

⋀   knit 3 tog (slip 1, k 2 tog, psso)

⋀   Slip 4 stitches (the number on the right side of the vertical line) to the right needle as if to purl, knit the next 5 stitches (the number on the left side), then pass the 4 slipped stitches over the 5 knitted stitches. It is often easier to slip these stitches one at a time.

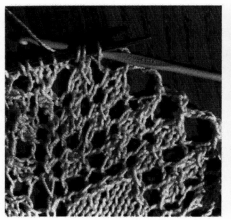
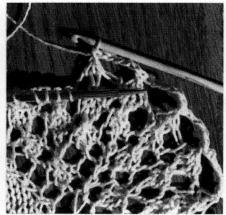
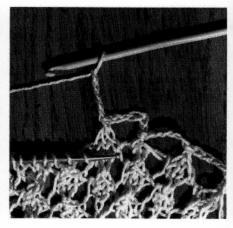

Fig. 9   Fig. 10   Fig. 11

[5]	Knit as many stitches tog as the number indicates (it may be easier to slip half of the stitches, knit remaining stitches tog, then pass the slipped stitches over).
⟵ 1M	Begin the round before the end of the interim row by as many stitches as the number indicates, moving the marker to correspond to the new starting point (i.e. move the beginning of the round to the right). Occasionally the new round will begin one or more stitches after the marker, moving the beginning of the row to the left. This will be noted on the individual pattern.
O O O = 11 M	from 3 yarn overs in the previous round, knit as many stitches as the number indicates
!	Attention – see explanations adjacent to chart
⟨↤	marks a change in the number of repeats per round
⑫	Crochet together into a single crochet stitch all knit stitches below the bracket, then crochet as many chain stitches as the number in the circle indicates

Knit all intermediate rows, twisting the twisted stitches. Exception: if there are several yarn overs in the previous round, then alternate knits and purls

Repeating the Basic Pattern, Repeats

All knitted tablecloths that are started in the center and knitted in rounds, including square ones, consist of a certain number of equal segments. The knitting chart is always written for only one segment, comparable to a slice of pie. In pieces knitted in the round the chart represents the pattern that has to be repeated in every round several times. The number of repetitions is determined by the design and is noted in the chart. You can see what happens when you knit one repeat too many in the individual round in the illustration on page 12. The tablecloth does not become bigger, only wider, so that it is more than a half circle when you fold it in the middle (*Fig. 8*). Such a tablecloth always has folds and never lies flat.

On page 25, 5 doilies are pictured which are composed of the same pattern elements, but in segments of different sizes, that is, the number of repeats of the pattern varies. The smallest doily, a square, consists of 4 segments, the oval of 8, and the round tablecloths of 6, 10, and (the largest) 12 segments. The chart, which is different for each doily, must be repeated accordingly [compare pp. 58-76.]

When a tablecloth has one or more borders in addition to the central part, then the number of necessary repeats may change from one part to another. Toward the edge, it can be twice or several times the original number. A change in the number of repeats is indicated in the charts and additionally is noted in the appropriate row.

Crochet Bind Off

After the last pattern row, a row of knit stitches (i.e. an intermediate row) is knitted, then the

Fig. 12

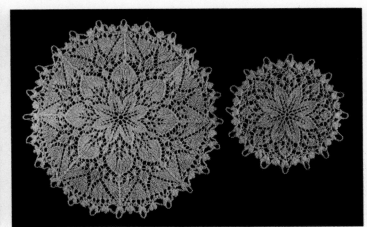

Fig. 13

15

stitches are crocheted off the circular knitting needle with a crochet hook. As illustrations 9 and 10 show, several knit stitches are crocheted together with a single crochet, then a small row of chain stitches is crocheted (*Fig. 11*) then again several knit stitches are taken onto the crochet hook into a single crochet stitch and so forth. The number of knit stitches to be combined (which can vary), and the number of chain stitches to be crocheted in between (which always remains the same), are given individually in the chart. In all examples in this collection, the crocheted edges are of the same size and unobtrusive.

The chain stitch loops are always formed with the same number of stitches (in almost all examples, 10 to 12) but you can also crochet more decorative edges, as for example the doily in illustration 13. In this case, each knitted stitch is crocheted off individually with a single crochet stitch, and an additional row of decorative crochet is added.

The doily in figure 12 is not well crocheted off. Too few knitted stitches are combined in each single crochet, but there are too many chain stitches in the arches. This is a pity. An otherwise balanced, cleanly worked doily appears sloppy.

Blocking

The completed tablecloths are given their finishing touch by blocking and light starching. Only through these techniques is the beautiful, regular pattern set off to best advantage.

For blocking, the outline of the tablecloth is copied onto paper or an old piece of linen, which is placed on a solid surface into which straight pins can be pushed. For doilies it is best to block on an ironing board, and for larger pieces, you can use the carpet. To begin with, pin the outer edges of the pattern segments with rust free pins, then add another pin to pull out each crocheted loop. Moisten the tablecloth with spray starch, let it dry, pull out the pins, and iron lightly.

Beware that blocking can result in tears if you pull on the cloth too hard. That is why you should first dry knitted tablecloths (as with all crocheted work) after laundering and block them when dry, moistening again with water or spray starch.

You can also change the shape of a tablecloth to a certain extent by blocking. For example, the oval tablecloth in the picture on p. 17 is originally round, as are all the other examples on that page, that is, it is worked with 8 equal segments. Instead of pinning the edges of each segment onto a circular line, this tablecloth was pulled longer on two opposite sides, then the remaining pins were placed on a previously traced oval outline.

Size: 82 cm (32") diameter; chart on pp. 52-55

Size: 72 cm (28") diameter; chart on pp. 72-73

Size: 150 cm (60") diameter; chart on pp. 28-29

19

Size: 100 cm (40") diameter; chart on pp. 34-35

20

Size: 58 cm (23") diameter; chart for a similar tablecloth on pp. 81-82

Size: 92 cm (36") diameter; chart on pp. 31-33

22

Size: 70 cm (28") diameter; chart on pp. 49-50

Doily on green cushion: 32 cm (13") diameter; chart on p. 64
Doily on brown cushion: 24 cm (10") diameter, chart on p. 26

24

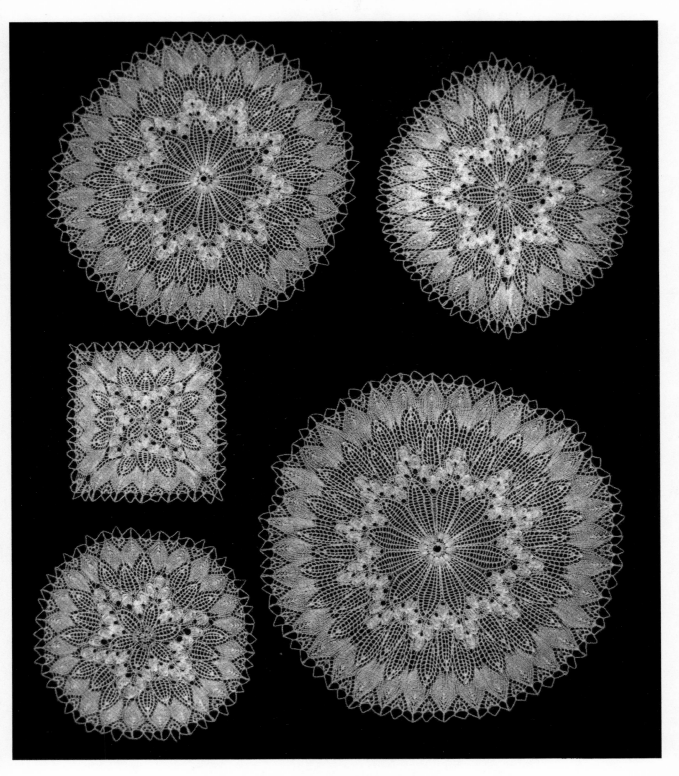

Pattern variations, charts on pp. 58-67

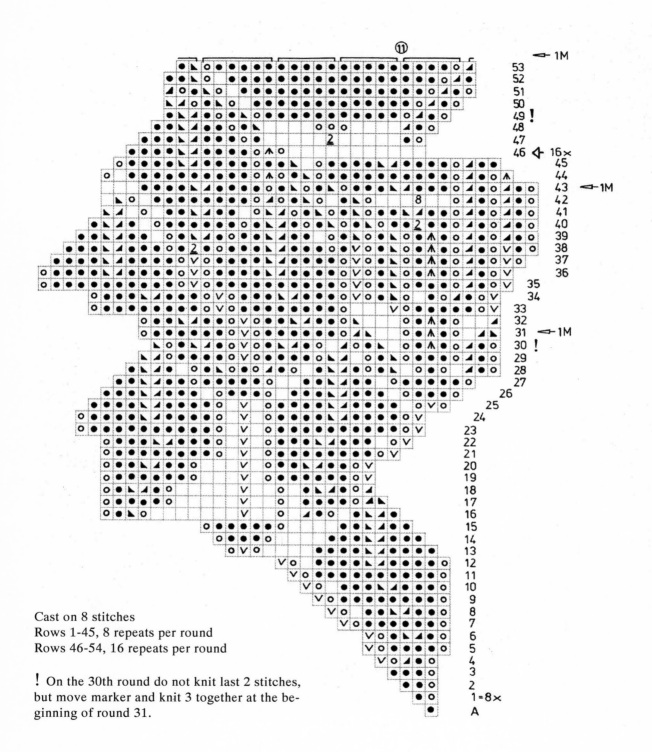

Cast on 8 stitches
Rows 1-45, 8 repeats per round
Rows 46-54, 16 repeats per round

! On the 30th round do not knit last 2 stitches,
but move marker and knit 3 together at the beginning of round 31.

Size: 24 cm (9") diameter (see color plate on p. 24); chart on p. 26;
5 gms #50 crochet thread; needle size 1.5 mm.

27

Rounds 122-126: knit.

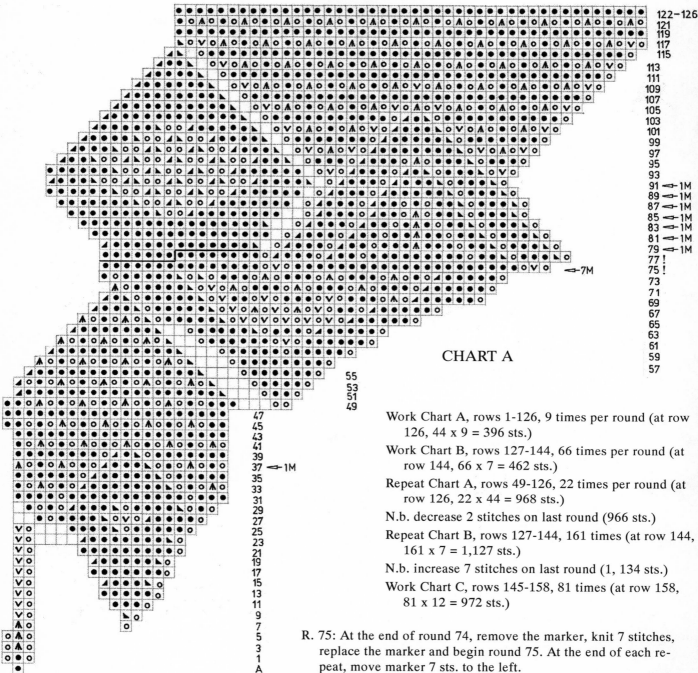

CHART A

Work Chart A, rows 1-126, 9 times per round (at row
  126, 44 x 9 = 396 sts.)

Work Chart B, rows 127-144, 66 times per round (at
  row 144, 66 x 7 = 462 sts.)

Repeat Chart A, rows 49-126, 22 times per round (at
  row 126, 22 x 44 = 968 sts.)

N.b. decrease 2 stitches on last round (966 sts.)

Repeat Chart B, rows 127-144, 161 times (at row 144,
  161 x 7 = 1,127 sts.)

N.b. increase 7 stitches on last round (1, 134 sts.)

Work Chart C, rows 145-158, 81 times (at row 158,
  81 x 12 = 972 sts.)

R. 75: At the end of round 74, remove the marker, knit 7 stitches,
  replace the marker and begin round 75. At the end of each repeat, move marker 7 sts. to the left.

R. 77: The last 15 stitches of each repeat are crossed as follows:
  Slip 8 sts. to a cable needle, hold in front of work. Knit the next
  7 sts., then knit the 8 sts. from the cable needle.

Cast on 9 stitches
9 repeats per round

28

Size: 150 cm (60") diameter; (see color plate on p. 19) chart on pp. 28-29;
300 gms #10 crochet thread; needle size 3.00 mm.

CHART C

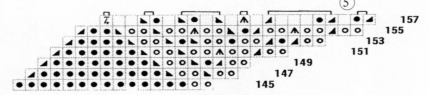

Repeat rounds 31-144.

Rounds 140-144: knit.

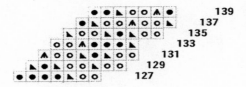

Size: 92 cm (36") diameter (see color plate on p. 22); chart on pp. 31-33;
80 gms #60 crochet thread; needle size 1.5 mm.

Chart continued on pp. 32-33

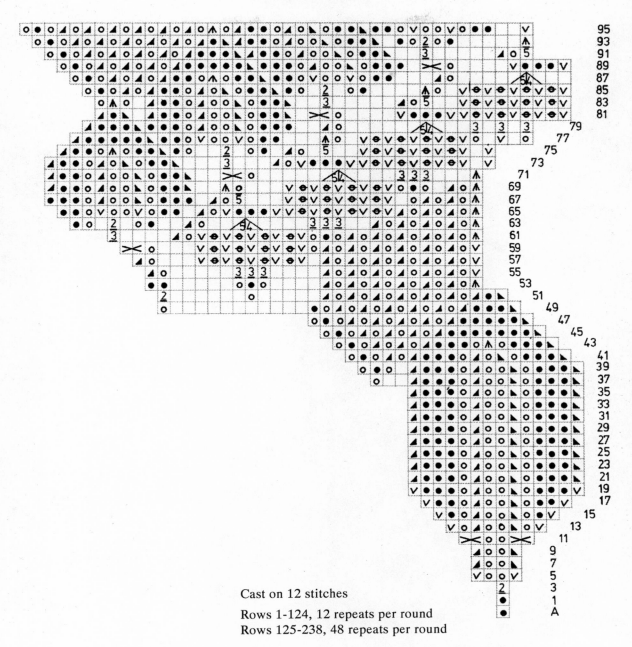

95
93
91
89
87
85
83
81
79
77
75
73
71
69
67
65
63
61
59
57
55
53
51
49
47
45
43
41
39
37
35
33
31
29
27
25
23
21
19
17
15
13
11
9
7
5
3
1
A

Cast on 12 stitches

Rows 1-124, 12 repeats per round
Rows 125-238, 48 repeats per round

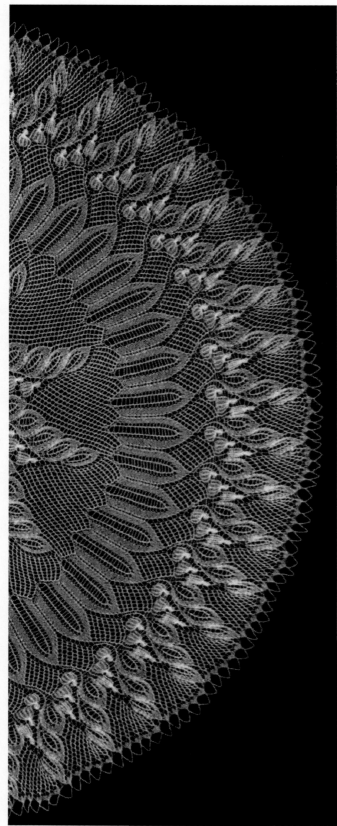

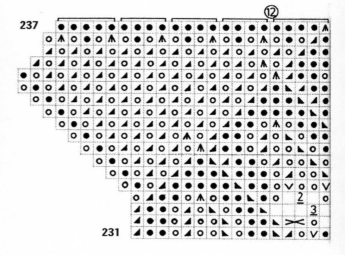

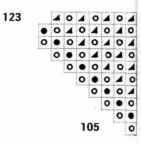

32

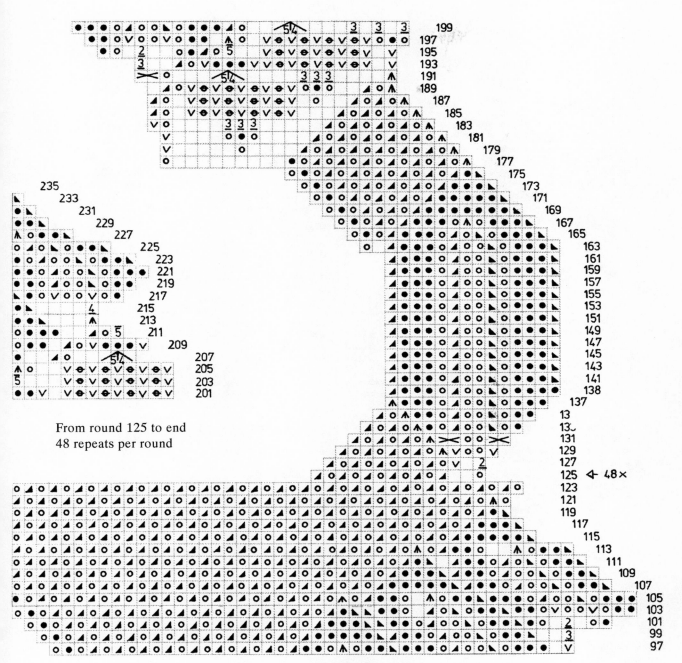

From round 125 to end
48 repeats per round

Continuation of chart from p. 31

199
197
195
193
191
189
187
185
183
181
179
177
175
173
171
169
167
165
163
161
159
157
155
153
151
149
147
145
143
141
138
137
13
13
131
129
127
125 ← 48×
123
121
119
117
115
113
111
109
107
105
103
101
99
97

235
233
231
229
227
225
223
221
219
217
215
213
211
209
207
205
203
201

33

Chart continued on p. 35

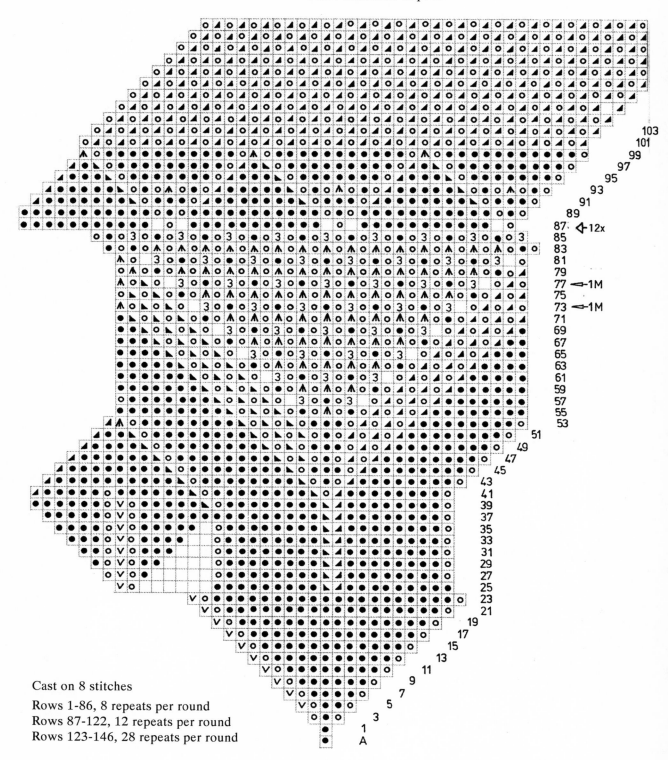

Cast on 8 stitches

Rows 1-86, 8 repeats per round
Rows 87-122, 12 repeats per round
Rows 123-146, 28 repeats per round

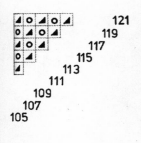

121
119
117
115
113
111
109
107
105

*Size: 100 cm(40")
diameter (see color
plate on p. 20);*

chart on pp. 34-35;

*120 gms #80 crochet
thread;
needle size 2 mm.*

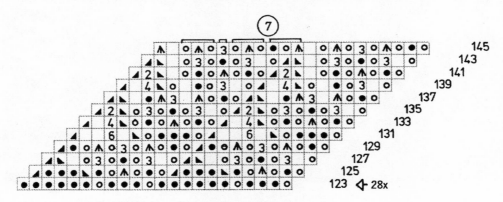

145
143
141
139
137
135
133
131
129
127
125
123 ◁ 28x

Continuation of chart from p. 34

Size: 19 cm (7-1/2") diameter;
10 gms #60 crochet thread; needle size 2 mm.

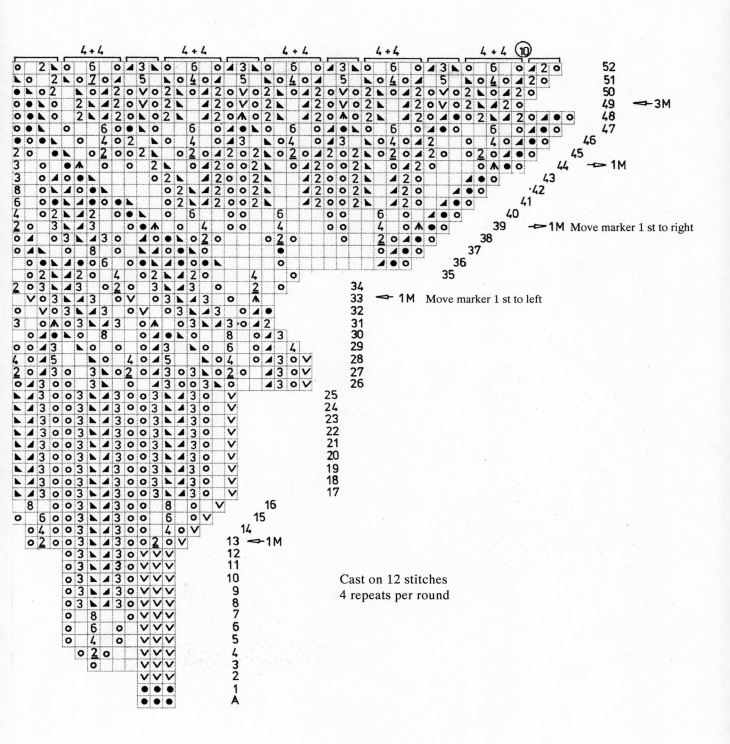

Cast on 12 stitches
4 repeats per round

Above: Size: 24 cm (9-1/2") diameter; charts A and B, then C on pp. 40-41;
10 gms #100 crochet thread; needle size 1.5 mm.

Left: Size 23 x 37 cm (9 x 14-1/2"); chart and diagram "A" (p. 40), then chart "C" on pp. 40-41;
25 gms #100 crochet thread; needle 1.5 mm; 3 circular needles or 2 sets of double point needles.

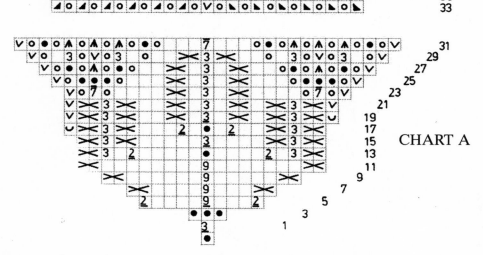

CHART B

CHART A

For round and oval tablecloths

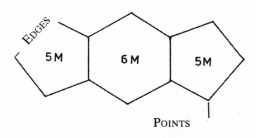

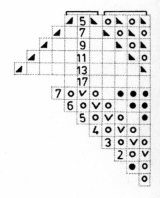

40

Oval Tablecloth with 8 Points, ill. p. 38:

Knit 3 individual doilies according to chart A. For 2 of the doilies, cast on 5 stitches and repeat the chart 5 times per round. For the third doily, cast on 6 stitches and repeat chart 6 times per round. After the 32nd round, the 3 doilies are sewn together as the diagram indicates, stitch to stitch. The rest of the stitches remain on the needles and are transferred to a single circular needle on the next round. The edge is worked according to chart C. *N.B.: the chart has variable repeats.* As can be seen from the diagram, the oval doily has 8 points and 12 sides. In chart C, the edge stitches are to the right of the bold line, and the point stitches are to the left of the bold line.

Begin knitting chart C at the point indicated in the diagram, and continue counterclockwise, alternating edges and points according to the diagram, that is, 1 edge, 1 point, 1 edge, 1 point, 2 edges, 1 point, etc.

Round Tablecloth, ill. p. 39:

Cast on 6 stitches and repeat chart A 6 times per round. After the 32nd round, knit chart B 6 times (rounds 33-38), then finish tablecloth with chart C, also repeating 6 times per round.

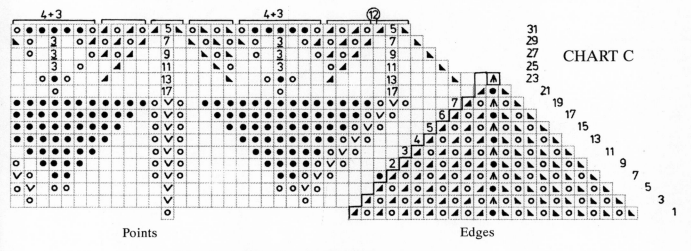

Edge for round and oval tablecloths

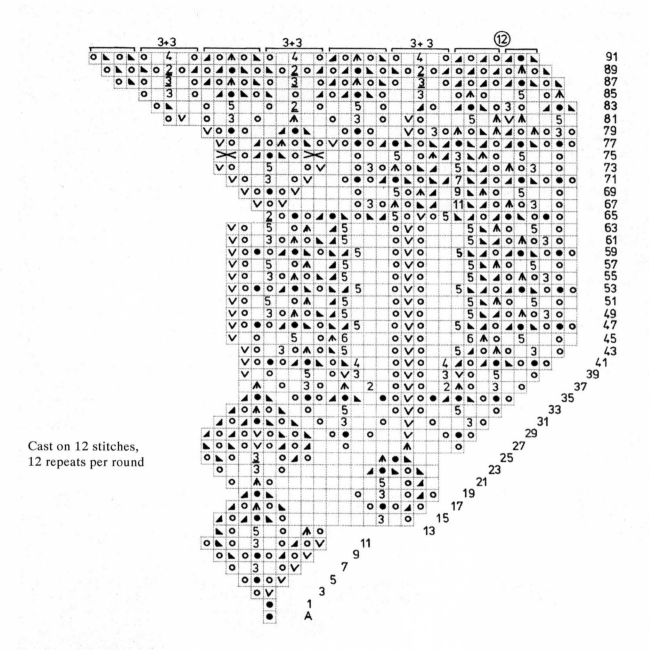

Cast on 12 stitches,
12 repeats per round

42

Size: 40 cm (16") diameter; chart to the left; 20 gms #60 crochet thread; needle size 1.5 mm.

Size: 68 cm (27") diameter; chart on pp. 45-47; 70 gms #60 crochet thread; needle size 1.5 mm.

Chart continued on pp. 46-47

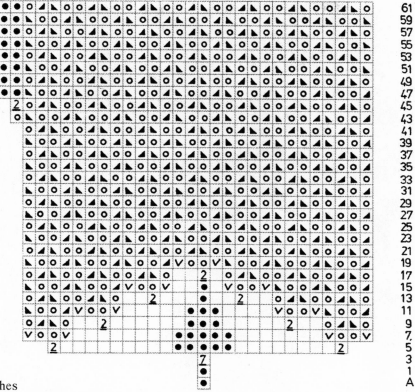

Cast on 8 stitches

Rows 1-158, 8 repeats per round
Rows 159-164, 96 repeats per round

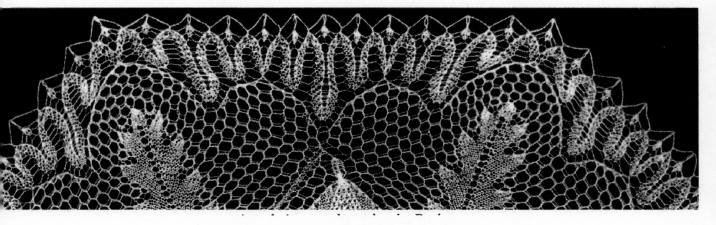

Detail of tablecloth shown on opposite page

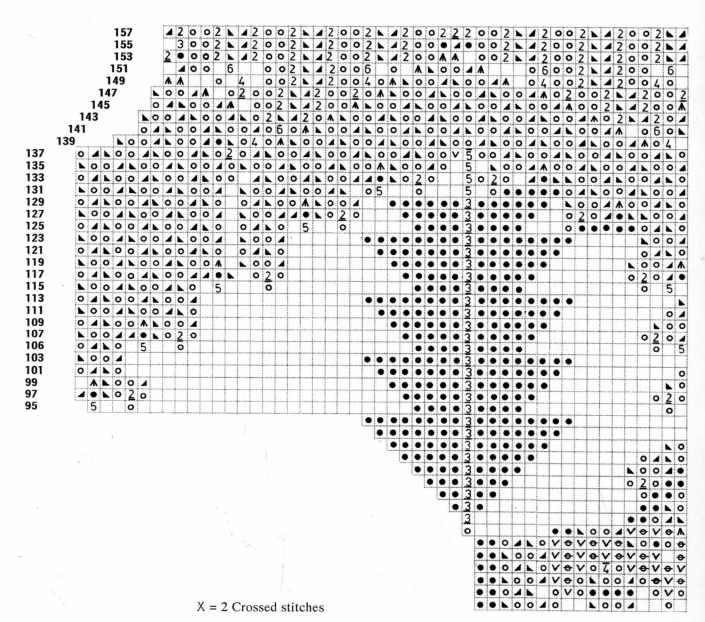

X = 2 Crossed stitches

Continuation of chart from p. 45

46

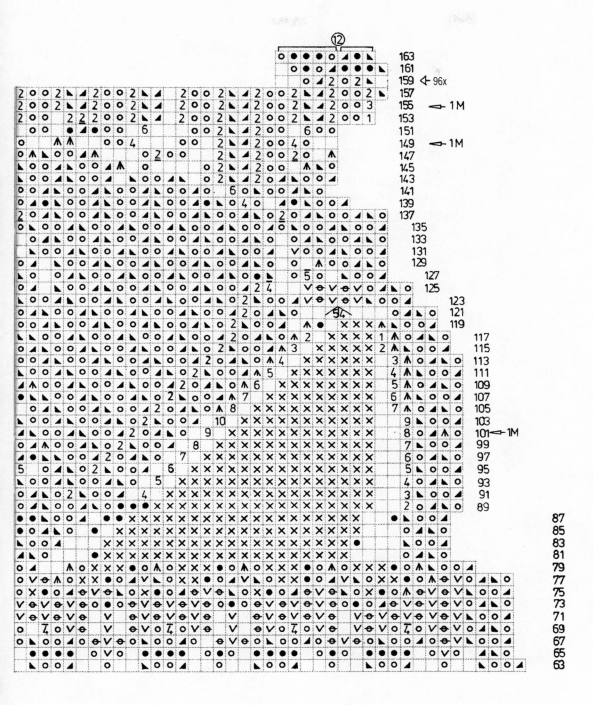

163
161
159 ← 96x
157
155 ← 1M
153
151
149 ← 1M
147
145
143
141
139
137
135
133
131
129
127
125
123
121
119
117
115
113
111
109
107
105
103
101 ← 1M
99
97
95
93
91
89
87
85
83
81
79
77
75
73
71
69
67
65
63

47

*Size: 70 cm (28") diameter (see color plate on p. 17); chart on pp. 49-50;
60 gms #30 crochet thread; needle size 2 mm.*

48

Chart continued on p. 50

Rounds 60-66, knit

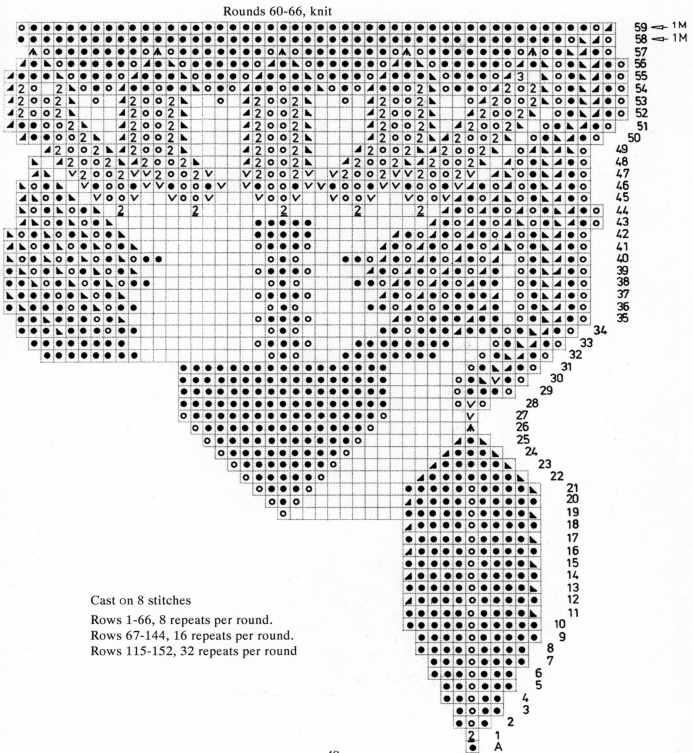

Cast on 8 stitches

Rows 1-66, 8 repeats per round.
Rows 67-144, 16 repeats per round.
Rows 115-152, 32 repeats per round

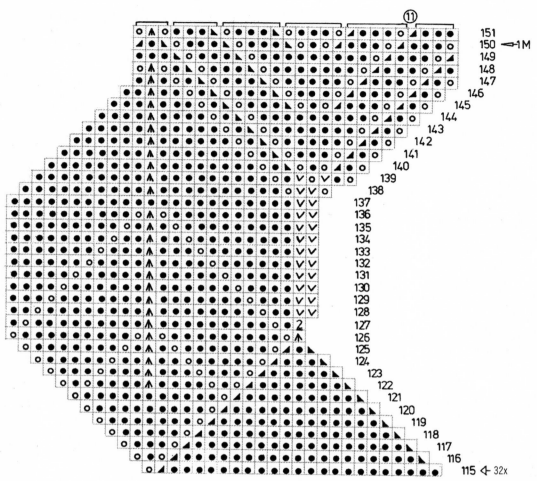

Rounds 108-114, knit
Repeat rounds 35-60

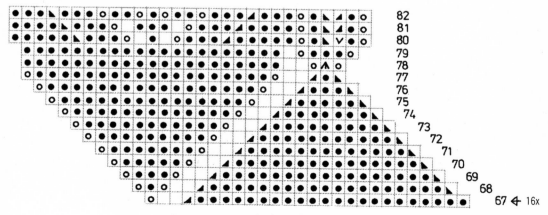

Continuation of Chart from p. 49

50

Size: 82 cm (32") diameter (see color plate on p. 17); chart on pp. 52-55;
80 gms #60 crochet thread; needle size 2 mm.

51

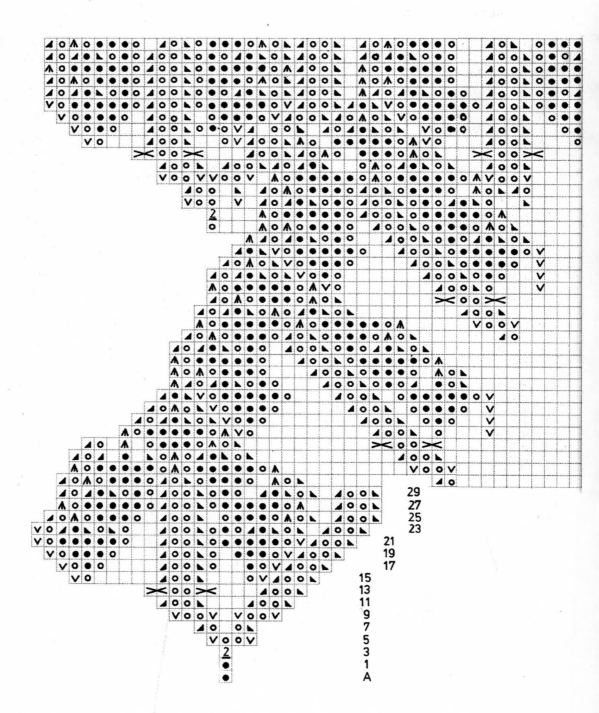

29
27
25
23

21
19
17

15
13
11
9
7
5
3
1
A

52

Chart continued on pp. 54-55.

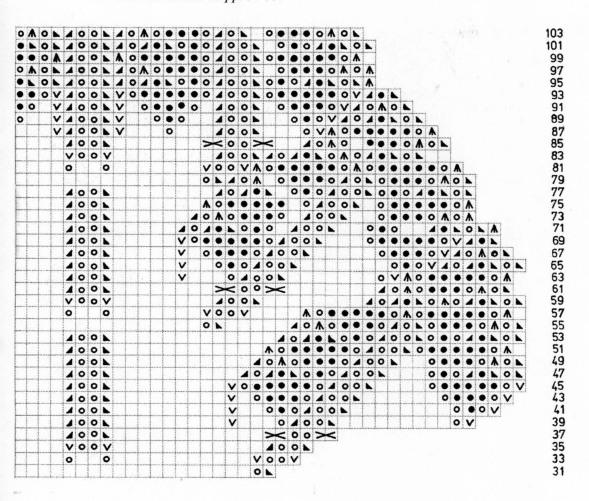

Cast on 8 stitches

Work rows 1-104 once per repeat (8 repeats per round).

! Rows 105-120: Work stitches between bold lines once, then work stitches after bold line twice for each repeat.

! Rows 121-214: Work 16 repeats per round.

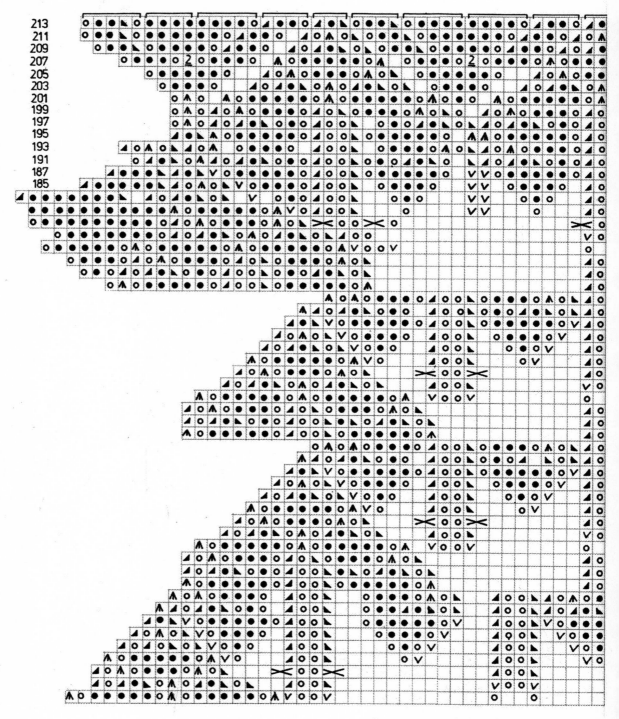

213
211
209
207
205
203
201
199
197
195
193
191
187
185

Continuation of chart from pp. 52-53

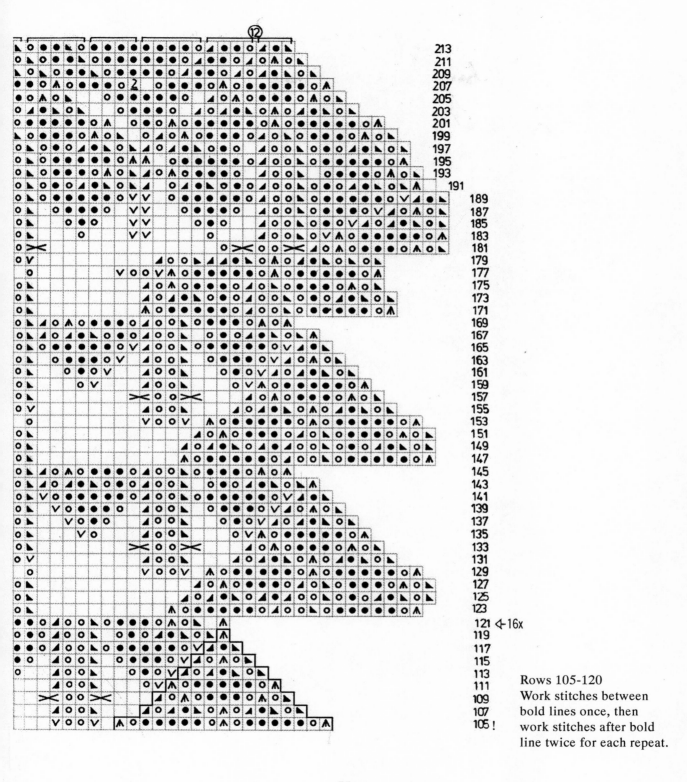

213
211
209
207
205
203
201
199
197
195
193
191

189
187
185
183
181
179
177
175
173
171
169
167
165
163
161
159
157
155
153
151
149
147
145
143
141
139
137
135
133
131
129
127
125
123

121 ⟵16x
119
117
115
113
111
109
107
105 !

Rows 105-120
Work stitches between
bold lines once, then
work stitches after bold
line twice for each repeat.

Rounds 80-84, knit

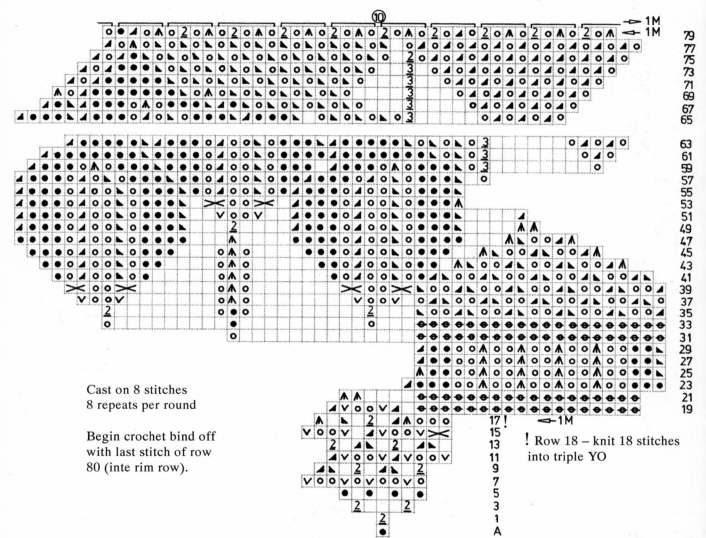

79
77
75
73
71
69
67
65

63
61
59
57
55
53
51
49
47
45
43
41
39
37
35
33
31
29
27
25
23
21
19

17 !
15
13
11
9
7
5
3
1
A

Cast on 8 stitches
8 repeats per round

Begin crochet bind off
with last stitch of row
80 (inte rim row).

! Row 18 – knit 18 stitches
into triple YO

Size: 28 cm (11") diameter; chart on p. 56; 10 gms #80 crochet thread; needle size 1.5 mm.

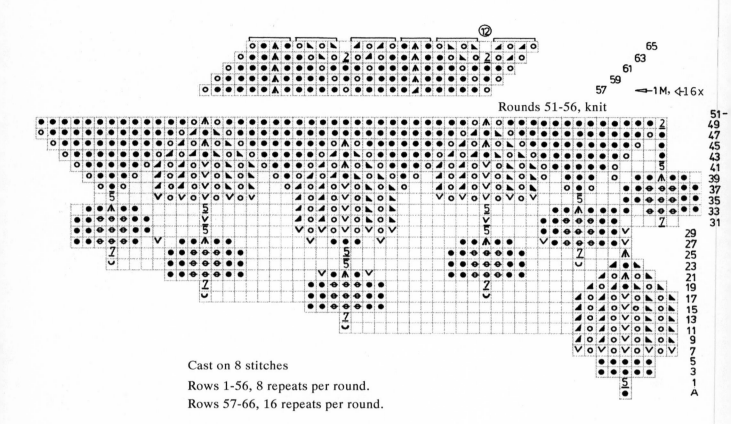

Rounds 51-56, knit

Cast on 8 stitches

Rows 1-56, 8 repeats per round.

Rows 57-66, 16 repeats per round.

Right: Size 27 cm (11") diameter (eight-pointed star).
The tablecloth was blocked as an oval, 31 cm (12") long (see ill. on p. 25);
chart above; 10 gms #60 crochet thread; needle size 1.5 mm.

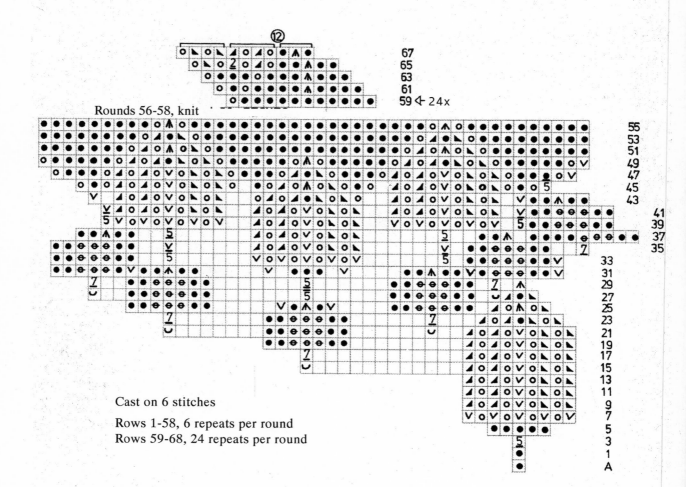

Rounds 56-58, knit

67
65
63
61
59 ⬐ 24x

55
53
51
49
47
45
43

41
39
37
35

33
31
29
27
25
23
21
19
17
15
13
11
9
7
5
3
1
A

Cast on 6 stitches

Rows 1-58, 6 repeats per round
Rows 59-68, 24 repeats per round

Size: 23 cm (9") diameter (six-pointed star); see ill. on p. 25; chart on p. 60;
8 gms #60 crochet thread; needle size 1.5 mm.

SQUARE DOILY

Size: 17 x 17 cm (6-1/2" sq); see ill. on p. 25;
5 gms #60 crochet thread; needle size 1.5 mm.

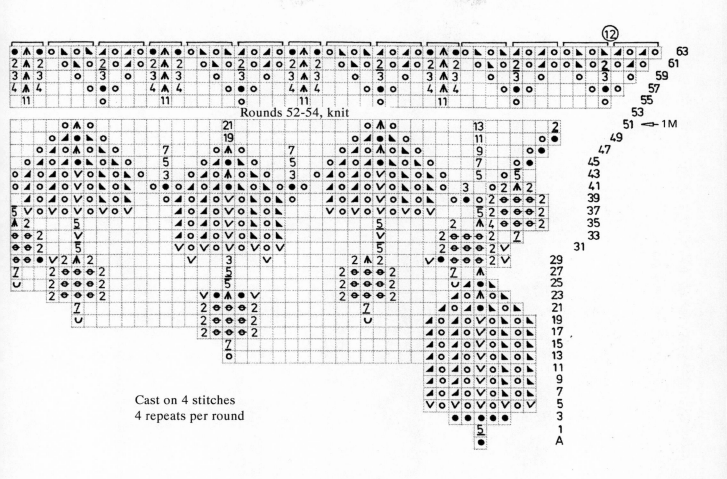

Rounds 52-54, knit

Cast on 4 stitches
4 repeats per round

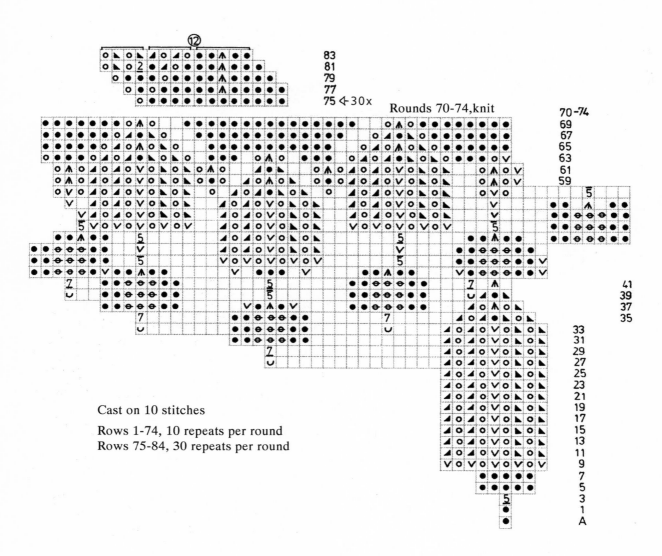

83
81
79
77
75 ⟵30x

Rounds 70-74, knit

70-74
69
67
65
63
61
59

57
55
53
51
49
47
45
43

41
39
37
35

33
31
29
27
25
23
21
19
17
15
13
11
9
7
5
3
1
A

Cast on 10 stitches

Rows 1-74, 10 repeats per round
Rows 75-84, 30 repeats per round

Size: 32 cm (12-1/2") diameter (ten-pointed star); see also ill. on p. 25; chart on p. 67;
12 gms #60 crochet thread; needle size 1.5 mm.

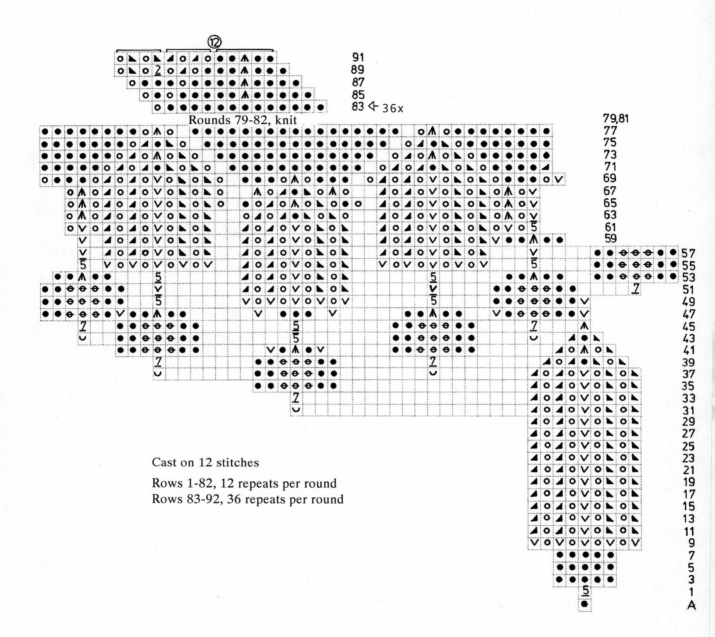

Cast on 12 stitches

Rows 1-82, 12 repeats per round
Rows 83-92, 36 repeats per round

Size: 36 cm (14") diameter (twelve-pointed star); see also ill. on p. 25; chart on p. 66; 15 gms #60 crochet thread; needle size 1.5 mm.

Size: 31 cm (12") diameter; chart on pp. (69-70);
10 gms #80 crochet thread; needle size 1.5 mm.

Chart continued on p. 70

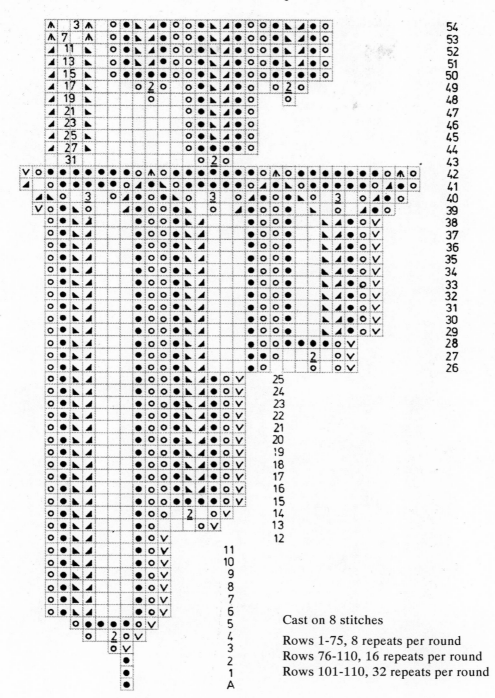

Cast on 8 stitches

Rows 1-75, 8 repeats per round
Rows 76-110, 16 repeats per round
Rows 101-110, 32 repeats per round

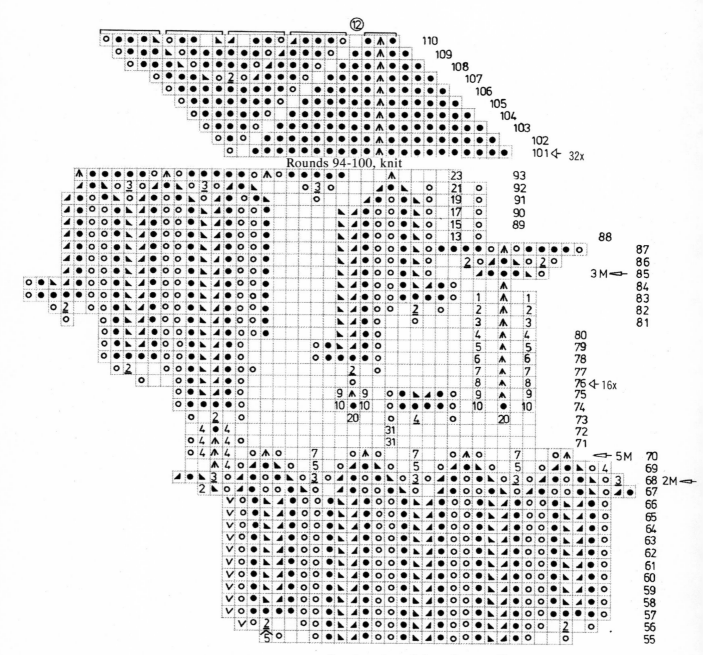

Rounds 94-100, knit

Continuation of chart from p. 69

70

Size: 72 cm (28") diameter; (see color plate on p. 18); chart on pp.72-73;
70 gms #60 crochet thread; needle size 1.5 mm.

Repeat rows 31-83

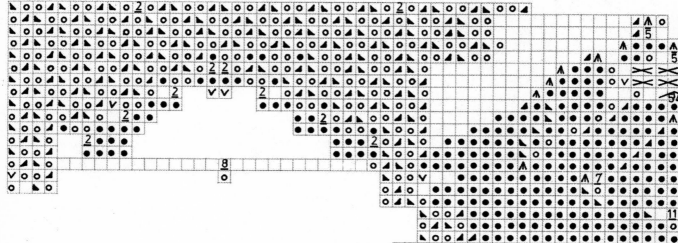

Cast on 8 stitches

Rows 1-144, 8 repeats per round
Rows 145-177, 32 repeats per round

Work rows 1-88;
repeat rows 31-83 (= rows 89-142), 16 times;
then work rows 143-178, 32 times.

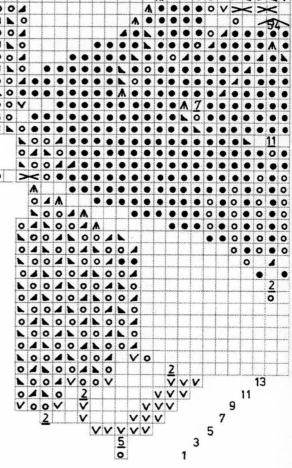

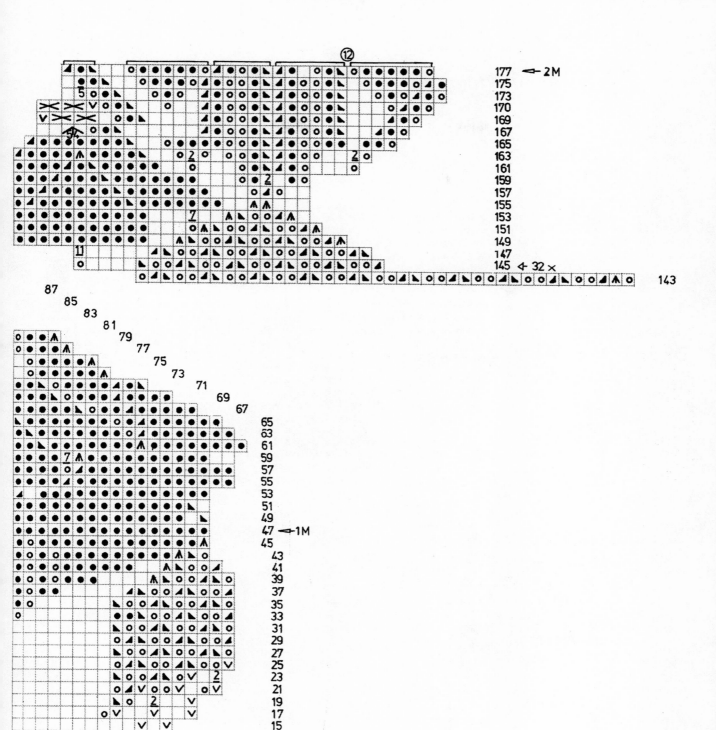

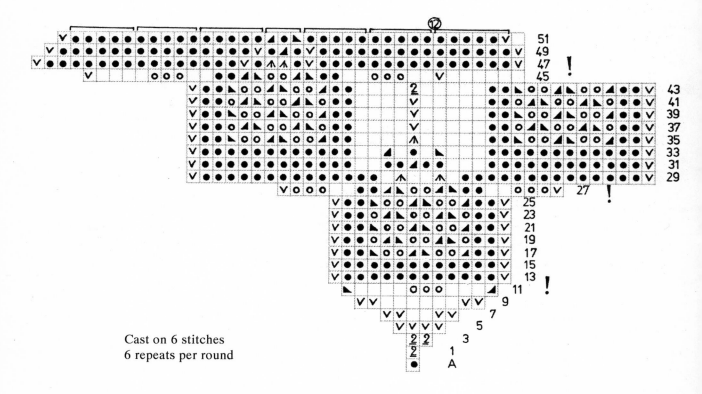

Cast on 6 stitches
6 repeats per round

In rounds 12 and 28, knit 12 stitches
into each triple YO

In round 46, knit 15 stitches into each
triple YO

Size: 23 cm (9") diameter; chart on p. 74; 10 gms #60 crochet thread; needle size 2 mm.

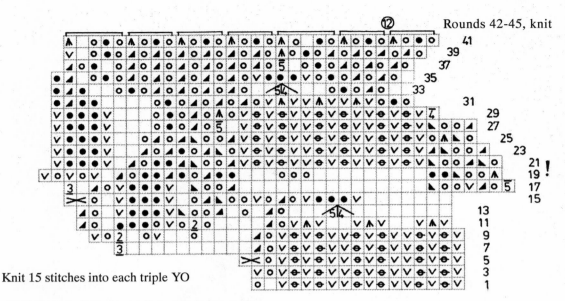

Rounds 42-45, knit

Knit 15 stitches into each triple YO

Begin with the crocheted center: chain 6, join into a ring.

1st round: 1 sc in ring, chain 12. Repeat 10 times. 1 sc in ring, join to first sc of round with 6 chain stitches and a double treble crochet.

2nd round: 1 sc in final chain loop (the loop just made), chain 12. Sc in next chain loop, chain 12. Repeat 9 times. 1 sc in last chain loop, join to first sc of round with 6 chain stitches and a treble crochet.

3rd round: 1 sc into final chain loop. Chain 12, 1 sc in next chain loop, chain 12, sc again into same loop. Repeat 10 times. Chain 12, sc into first loop, join to first sc of round with 6 chain stitches and a treble crochet.

4th round: 1 sc in final chain loop, chain 12. Sc in next chain loop, chain 12. Repeat 21 times. 1 sc in last chain loop, join to first sc of round with 6 chain stitches and a treble crochet.

5th round: join final chain loop to the first chain loop by making 1 sc into both loops at once, chain 16; join next 2 chain loops together with 1 sc, chain 16. Repeat 9 times. Join last 2 chain loops together with 1 sc, join to first sc of round with 8 chain stitches and a quadruple crochet.

6th round: 1 sc in final chain loop, chain 16. Repeat 10 times. 1 sc in last chain loop, join to first sc of round with 16 chain stitches.

Now you have 12 chain stitch loops. Without breaking thread, knit 15 stitches into each chain stitch loop and begin knitting chart.

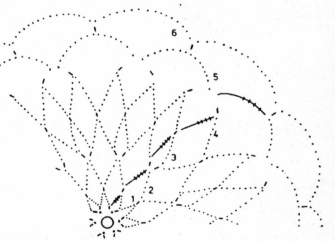

Crochet Symbols:
- chain stitch
- single crochet
- double treble crochet (thread 3x around hook)
- triple treble crochet (thread 4x around hook)

76

Size: 22 cm (9") diameter; chart for crochet and knitting on p. 76
10 gms #60 crochet thread; crochet hook and circular needle in size 1.5 mm.

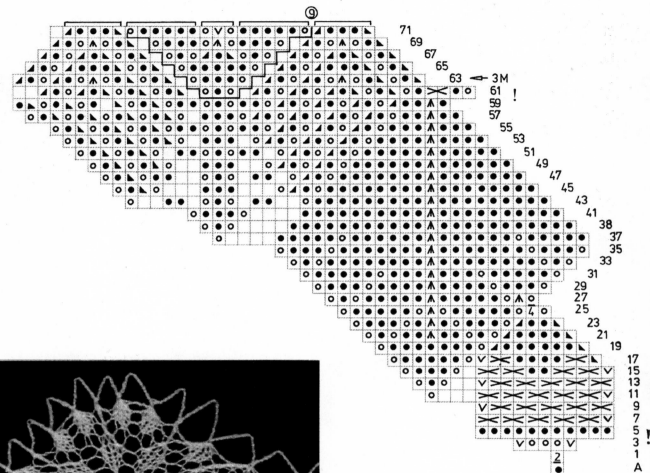

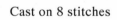

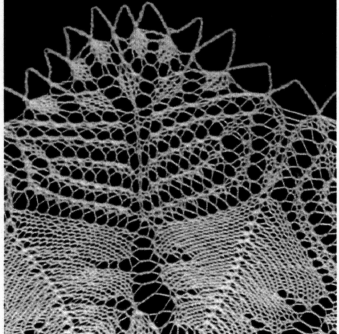

Detail

Cast on 8 stitches

8 Repeats per round
In round 4, knit 9 stitches into each triple YO
! Repeat stitches between bold lines (rows 61-71)
  twice in each repeat.

78

Size: 42 cm (16-1/2") diameter; chart and detail on p. 78;
20 gms #20 crochet thread; 39 cm (15-1/2") diameter with 10 gms #70 crochet thread;
needle size 1.5 mm in both cases.

Size: 58 cm (23") diameter; chart on pp. 81-82;
40 gms #40 crochet thread; needle size 1.5 mm.

Chart continued on p. 82

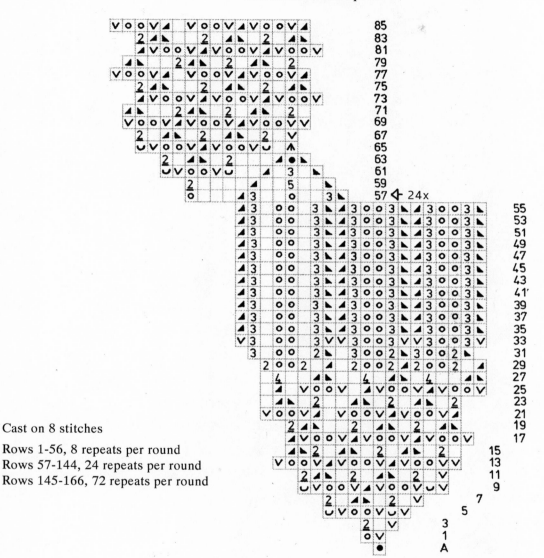

Cast on 8 stitches

Rows 1-56, 8 repeats per round
Rows 57-144, 24 repeats per round
Rows 145-166, 72 repeats per round

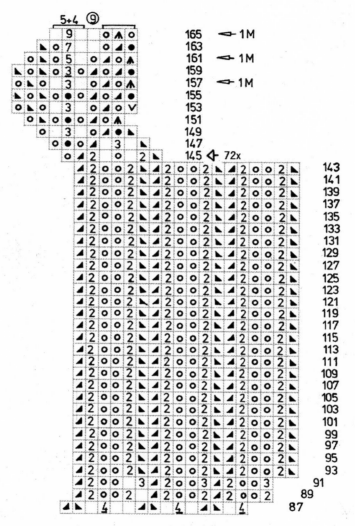

Continuation of chart from p. 81

Size: 49 cm (19") diameter; chart on pp. 84-85; 20 gms #60 crochet thread; needle size 2 mm.

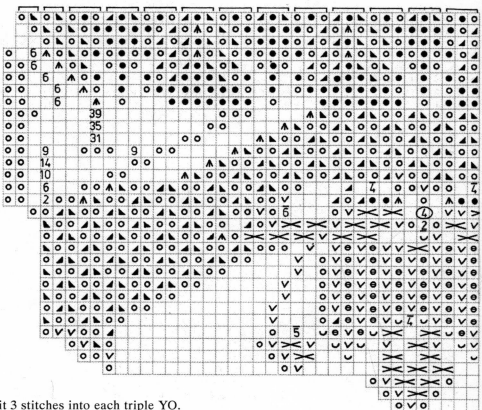

In round 44, knit 3 stitches into each triple YO.

In round 60, knit 9 stitches into each triple YO.

In round 66, knit 3 stitches into each triple YO.

In round 49- ④ knit 4 stitches onto a cable needle and wind yarn 20 times around those 4 stitches, then slip them onto right needle and continue as charted.

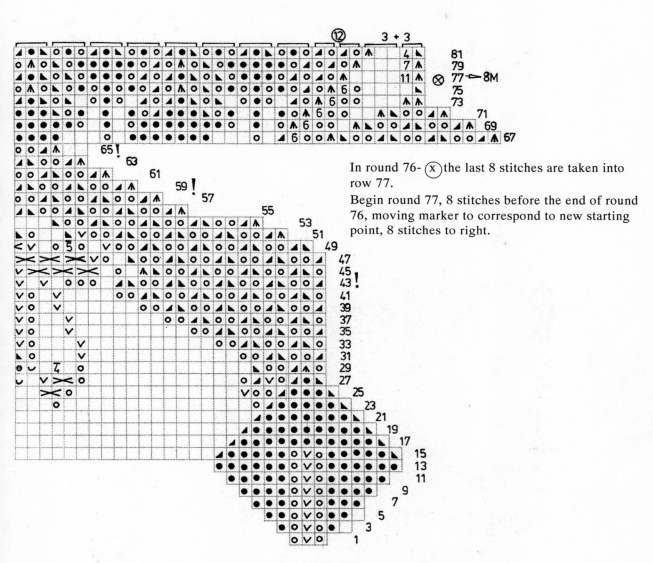

In round 76- (X) the last 8 stitches are taken into row 77.

Begin round 77, 8 stitches before the end of round 76, moving marker to correspond to new starting point, 8 stitches to right.

Cast on 6 stitches
6 repeats per round

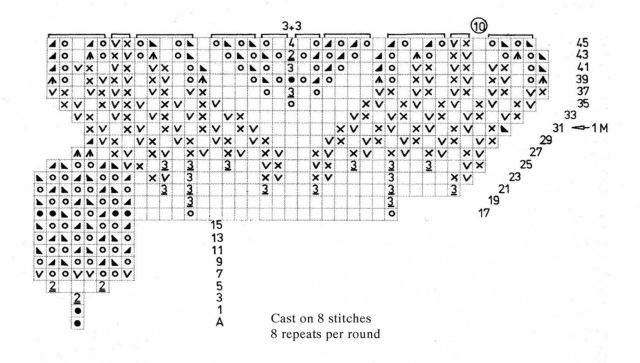

3+3   ⑩

45
43
41
39
37
35
33
31 ⟵ 1M
29
27
25
23
21
19
17

15
13
11
9
7
5
3
1
A

Cast on 8 stitches
8 repeats per round

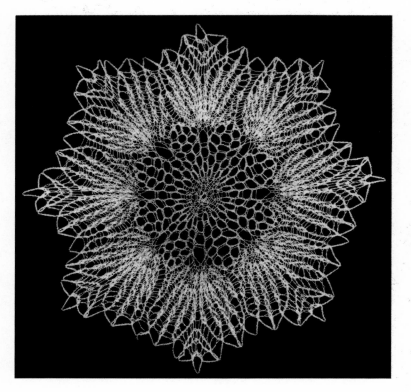

Size: 17 cm (7") diameter; chart above; 5 gms #100 crochet thread; needle size 1.5 mm.

Right:
Size: 40 x 80 cm (16" x 32"); chart on pp. 88-91;
40 gms #100 crochet thread; 2 sets of double point needles or 2 circular needles, size 1.5 mm.

This rectangular tablecloth is worked as 2 or more square doilies with a common edge. However many doilies are combined, the edge can be repeated as needed to fit.

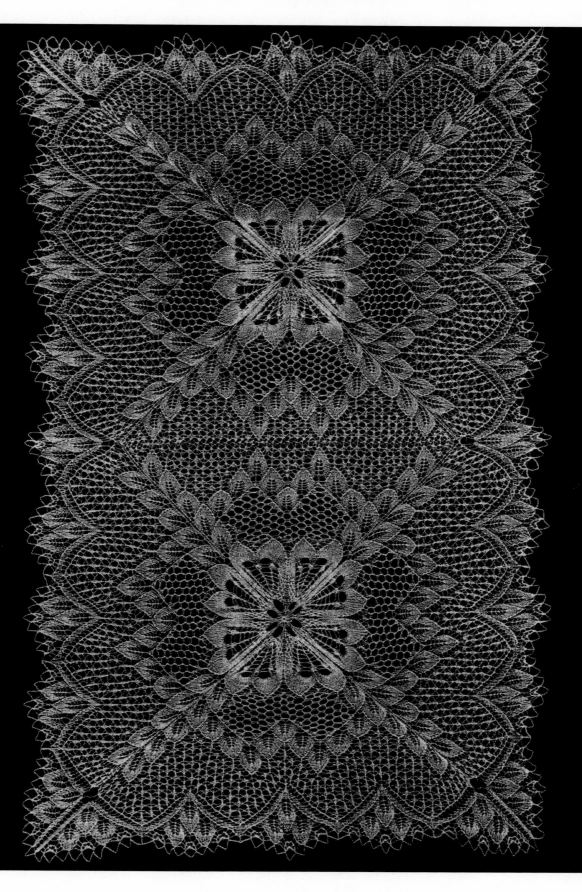

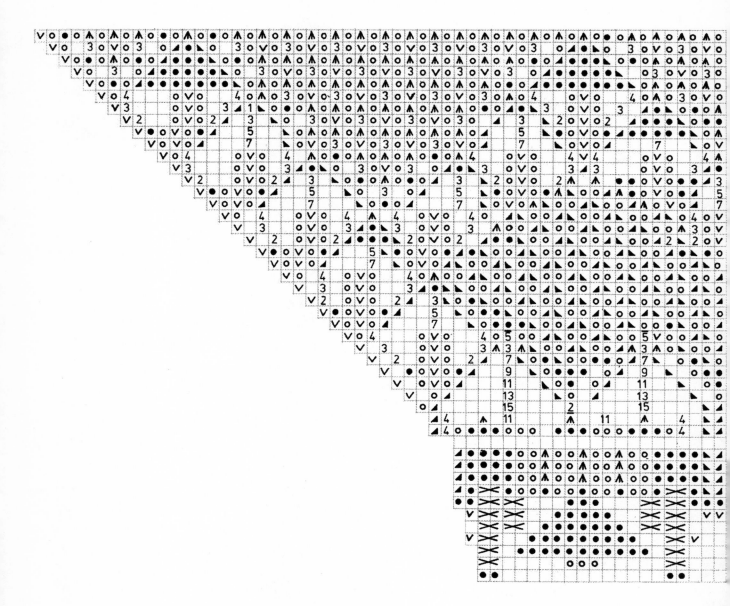

Chart continued on pp. 90-91.

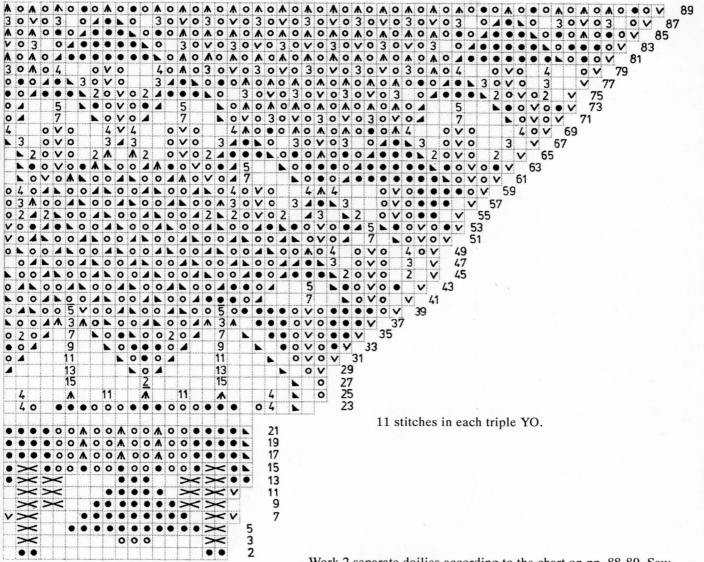

11 stitches in each triple YO.

Cast on 32 stitches
4 repeats per round

Work 2 separate doilies according to the chart on pp. 88-89. Sew together, stitch to stitch, along one side, to form a rectangle. The stitches from the other sides remain on the needles and are knitted onto a single circular needle in the first row of the edging (chart on pp. 90-91).

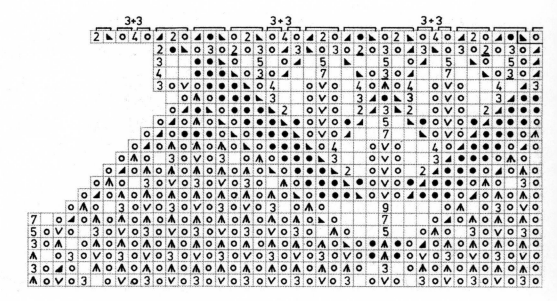

Continuation of chart from pp. 88-89.

N.B.: the chart for the edge has variable repetitions. Beginning at any corner of the combined doilies, work round 1, repeating the stitches to the left of the bold line for each scallop to fit the edge. On round 2, the stitches within bold lines on the right side of the chart are worked at the corner, then the stitches to the left of the line are repeated once for each scallop. Repeat these stitches 7 times for the long sides and 3 times for the short sides, working the corner stitches once in between sides. If 3 or more doilies are joined, the side stitches must be repeated as many times as necessary to fit.

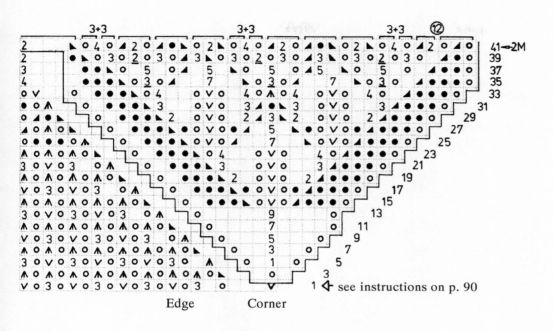

Edge   Corner

1 ⟵ see instructions on p. 90

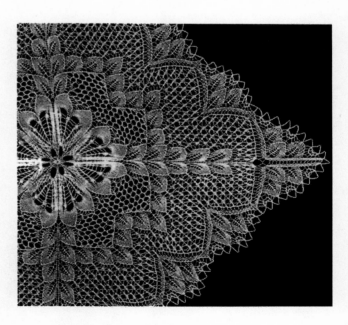

Detail of Tablecloth From p. 87

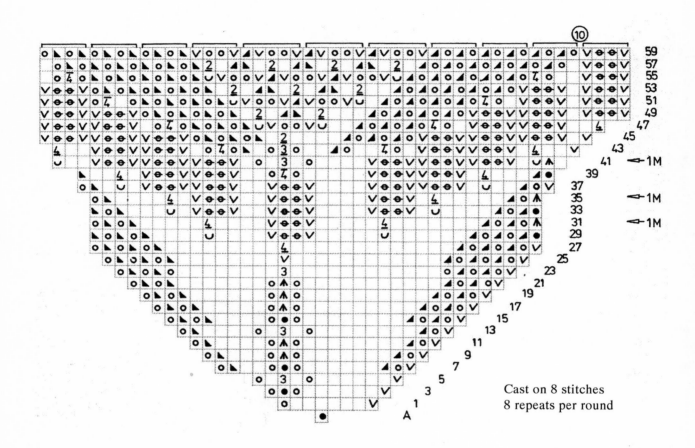

Cast on 8 stitches
8 repeats per round

59
57
55
53
51
49
47
45
43
41 ⟵1M
39
37
35 ⟵1M
33
31 ⟵1M
29
27
25
23
21
19
17
15
13
11
9
7
5
3
1
A

10

92

Size: 28 cm (11") diameter; chart on p. 92; 15 gms #60 crochet thread; needle size 1.5 mm.

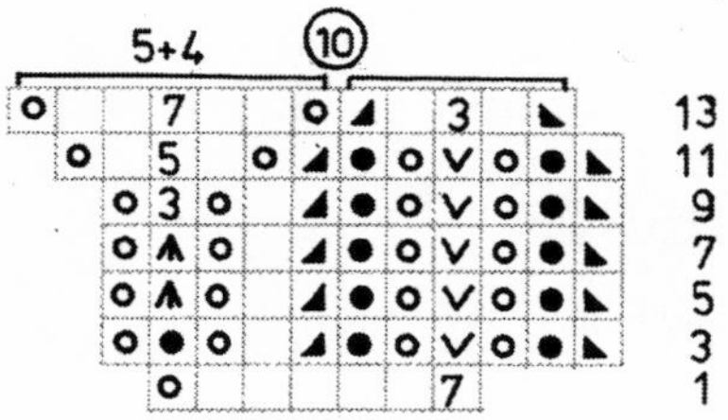

Chart C

Repeat 7 stitches and 1 YO into each crocheted loop from Chart B, and repeat Chart C 40 times per round

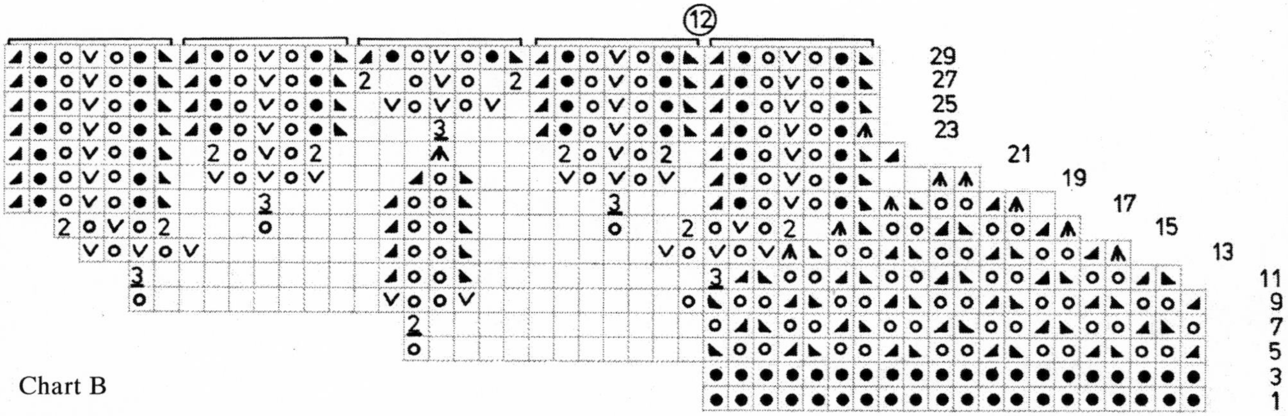

(10) 5+4 ... row numbers: 13, 11, 9, 7, 5, 3, 1

(12) ... row numbers: 29, 27, 25, 23, 21, 19, 17, 15, 13, 11, 9, 7, 5, 3, 1

Chart B

Knit 8 stitches into each crocheted loop from Chart A and repeat Chart B 8 times per round.

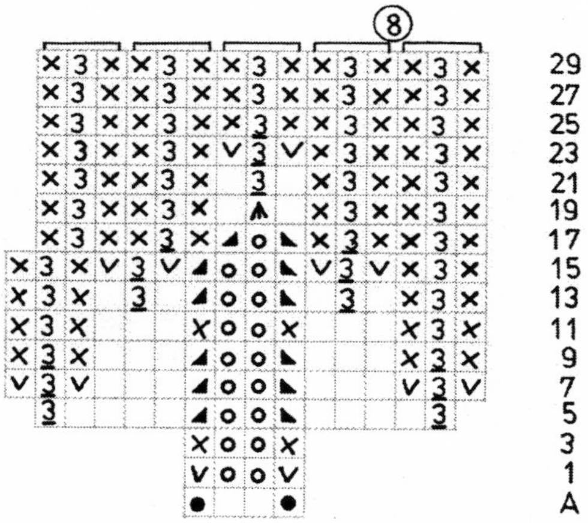

Chart A

Cast on 8 Stitches
4 repeats per round

(8) ... row numbers: 29, 27, 25, 23, 21, 19, 17, 15, 13, 11, 9, 7, 5, 3, 1, A

Note that each chart is crocheted off with chain stitch loops, and charts B and C begin by knitting into the loops of the preceding chart. For chart B, knit 8 stitches into each loop (8 stitches x 5 loops = 40 stitches. Chart B is repeated 8 times, twice for each segment of Chart A). For chart C, knit 7 stitches into each loop and make a YO between loops. (7 stitches + 1 YO x 5 loops = 40 stitches; repeat 40 times, 5 times for each segment of Chart B)

94

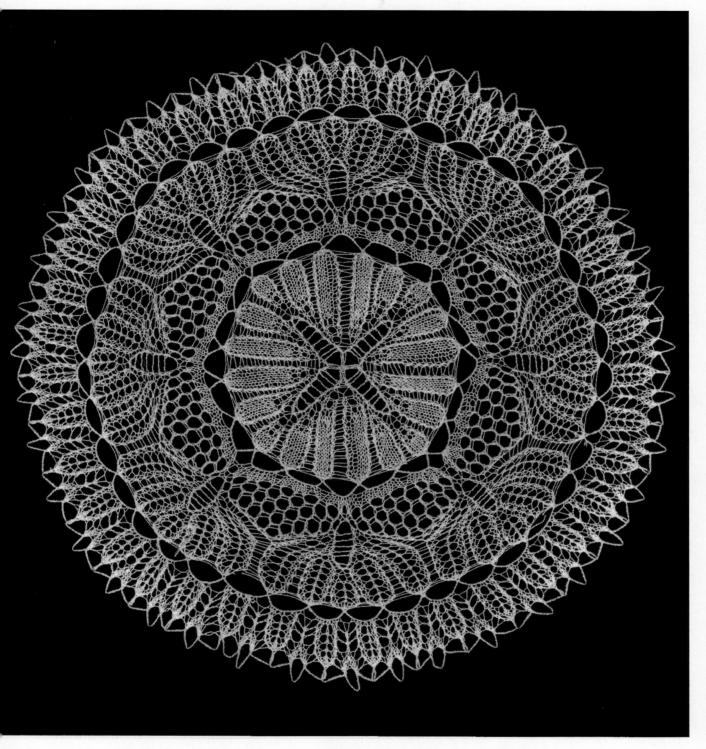

Size: 30 cm (12") diameter; charts on p. 94; 10 gms #80 crochet thread; needle size 1.5 mm.